H is for Hummingbirds

Written by Merry Bradshaw

Photographs by David Boyarski

Dedication

For Marc, Val and Kelly, my support team in all I do.
Merry

For Abby and Hailey, I hope this book inspires you to learn about nature.
For Jane, my most excellent spotter and life companion.
David

H is for Hummingbirds

Text Copyright © 2018 by Merry Bradshaw
Photographs Copyright © 2018 by David Boyarski

Softcover: ISBN 978-0-9995294-0-9
Hardcover: ISBN 978-0-9995294-1-6
eBook: ISBN 978-0-9995294-2-3

cedarpocketpress.com
cedarpocketpress@cedarpocketpress.com

Cedar
Pocket
Press

I AM A HUMMINGBIRD

I dart

I dash

I zig

I zag

I swoop

I flutter

I buzz

I hum

I zoom

I hover

I hunt

I search

I find

I see

A flower

Waiting

Just for me

Merry Bradshaw

A a

Acrobats

Forward, backwards, upside down
hummingbirds can fly.
Darting, dashing, diving,
acrobats in the sky.

Hummingbirds fly like no other bird. They fly forward, backward, sideways and upside down. When darting flower-to-flower searching for nectar, you may even see a hummingbird do a backward somersault. These *acrobatic* displays are due to a combination of certain physical characteristics. Their tiny bodies are helped by: hollow bones, large chest muscles, a solid backbone, small feet and a large heart. Flying at speeds of 20 to 45 mph while moving their wings more than 60 beats per second, makes hummingbirds truly *acrobats* in the sky.

Bill

When hummingbirds get hungry
and they look for food to eat,
they use their **bill** and tongue
to grab a tasty treat.

B b

Some hummingbirds' needle-like **bills** are straight, others curved. They vary in length from 8mm to 119mm or 4½ inches, easily reaching deep inside a flower. Hair and grooves on their long tongue capture the nectar for their meal. Amazingly, hummingbird tongues can dart in and out of a flower up to 13 times a second to extract the luscious nectar. Their long **bills** also help them pick tiny insects off plants and out of the air to eat.

C c

Camouflage

Hummingbird nests are hard to find,
mothers build them out of view.
Camouflaged to protect their young
with old twigs and leaves, not new.

Hummingbirds are loved for their
dazzling beauty. Their nests are just the
opposite and often hard to find.
Hummingbirds pick odd places to build
their tiny nests. Besides hiding them in
trees, you might see one in a prickly
cactus, wind chime or inside a porch
light. They use twigs, leaves, spider silk,
moss and even dryer lint to *camouflage*
their nests from predators.

D d

Daring

Hummingbirds can be quite daring, protecting their nest or food. Whether bird or bee or human watch out for their bad mood.

If you see a hummingbird quickly darting and diving back and forth, most likely they feel their nest or food source is being threatened. They are territorial and can be quite *daring* and aggressive when protecting their nest, feeder, or a flower. Besides buzzing around to shoo others away, hummingbirds also use some of these same fast movements to attract a mate.

E e

Eggs

Hummingbirds lay two tiny **eggs** each the size of a green pea. It takes 3 weeks before they hatch hairless, dark and quite hungry.

In a tiny nest the size of a ping-pong ball, a female hummingbird will lay two **eggs,** sometimes only one. The **eggs** are the size of a jellybean or a pea. After sitting on the **eggs** (incubating) for about 3 weeks, the baby hummingbirds will hatch. Born naked and with dark skin, they look more like a raisin than a baby bird.

Fledgling

When hummingbirds are 3 weeks old
they leave their tiny nest.
Mother will teach her fledglings now
which flowers are the best.

At about three weeks old baby hummingbirds leave the nest. They are called *fledglings*. Usually the babies *(fledglings)* fly to a nearby bush or tree where their mother will feed them for a few more days. She also shows them where to find good bugs and flowers, so they will soon be able to eat on their own.

G g

Gorget

See the brilliant feathers
sparkle around their neck?
Purple, green, red or blue,
look at those gorgets!

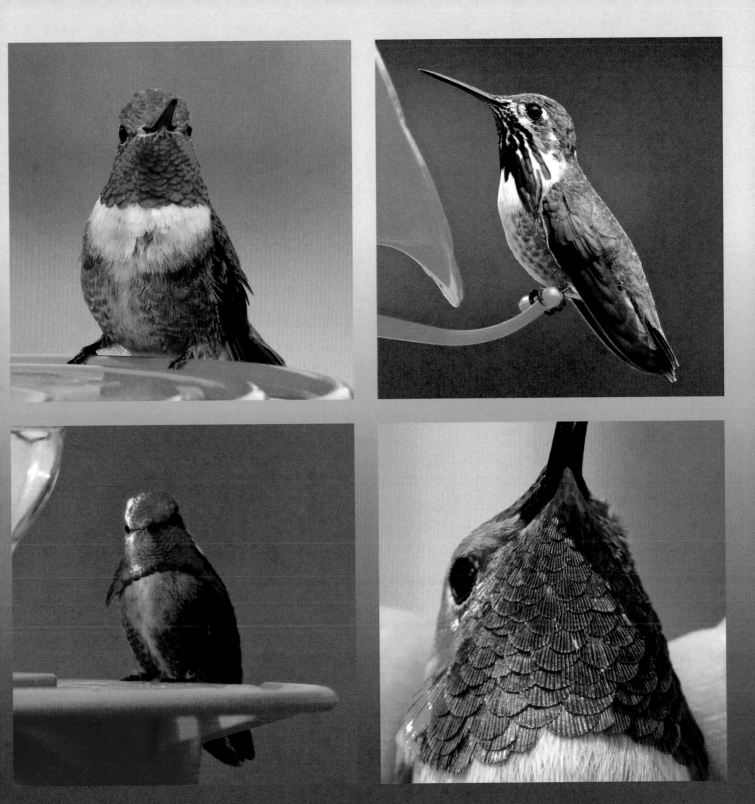

Male hummingbirds look very showy with their brilliant colored throat feathers called a ***gorget***. This word comes from the days when a knight-in-armor wore a metal collar to protect his throat. Hummingbirds' ***gorgets*** are eye-popping in iridescent colors of purple, pink, red, orange, blue and green. Which color do you like the best?

H h

Hover

Hummingbirds don't always sit to eat,
they hover in one place.
Drawing out sweet nectar,
wings moving at rapid pace.

Hummingbirds are unique! Their wing structure allows them to not only fly backwards and forwards, but also **hover** in place. Their wings rotate in a figure eight rather than flap like other birds. This is useful when they dash and dart from one flower to another. Rather than resting on a branch, they will **hover** at each flower to eat bugs or drink nectar.

Ii

Iridescence

Sparkling, dazzling, shiny and bright,
hummingbird feathers are a
stunning delight.
Brilliant colors that flicker in light,
iridescent reflections that please
our sight.

We love the bright and shiny colored feathers of hummingbirds. What you see is called *iridescence*. Usually these shimmering feathers are on the throat or chest of a male hummingbird. The colorful sheen occurs because of the feathers' structure and how they reflect light. The feathers themselves are not the beautiful colors you see. Only when the sun shines on the feathers at just the right angle can we see the spectacular colors.

J j

Jewel

Feathers colored like precious jewels
hummingbirds are special to see,
in emerald, amethyst,
sapphire or brilliant ruby.

Hummingbirds' *jewel-like* colors keep many of us hoping to catch a glimpse of one as it darts around a garden or feeder. Their bright iridescent feathers make us think of jewels like rubies, sapphires and emeralds. The names of some hummingbirds tell you how *jewel-like* their appearance really is: Andean Emerald, Ruby-throated, Sapphire-bellied, Emerald-chinned, Blue-head Sapphire or Amethyst Woodstar

K k

Kaleidoscope

Turn, turn your **kaleidoscope**,
see colors change and pop.
Notice the pretty hummingbird
whose bright colors never stop.

A *kaleidoscope* is a tube that contains loose pieces of colored plastic or glass. The pieces are separated into sections between mirrors. Endless patterns of beauty are seen when the tube is turned. Hummingbirds may remind you of a *kaleidoscope* as you look at the many colors of a hummingbird from head to tail, on their belly and around their neck.

L l

Lifespan

Imagine tiny hummingbirds what they do to just survive. Their **lifespan** is surprising since many migrate throughout their lives.

A hummingbird's *lifespan* is an average 3 to 4 years. Some banded hummingbirds have been found to live 10 to 12 years or more. Newborn or fledgling hummingbirds are at the greatest risk of dying due to their delicate state. Some hummingbird species migrate across the ocean with the seasons and return year after year. How remarkable!

M m

Molt

Hummingbirds **molt** each year,
shabby and scruffy to see.
Old feathers gone, replaced with new,
now pretty and full as can be.

Feathers cannot be fixed or heal themselves if damaged. Similar to our hair, feathers fall out in a process called ***molt*** and new ones appear. ***Molt*** is important to keep hummingbird feathers in top flying condition. Hummingbirds usually ***molt*** twice a year. This 2 to 3 week process usually happens during seasonal changes. Sometimes hummingbirds will have different colored feathers after ***molting***. During ***molt***, hummingbirds look very raggedy until their new feathers grow out.

N n

Nectar

Hummers eat all day long.
Food gives them energy.
Flowers are their favorite
where nectar is sure to be.

The favorite food of a hummingbird is **_nectar_**. This sugary liquid inside a flower provides hummingbirds with the energy they need to live. Their long bills and grooved tongue help extract the sweet treat from deep inside the flower. They eat nearly twice their weight in **_nectar_** each day. It is easy to understand why we see hummingbirds darting from flower to flower so quickly. What big appetites they have!

Ornithologist

Scientists study many things.
Ornithologists like birds the best.
They learn about each species
and what's different from the rest.

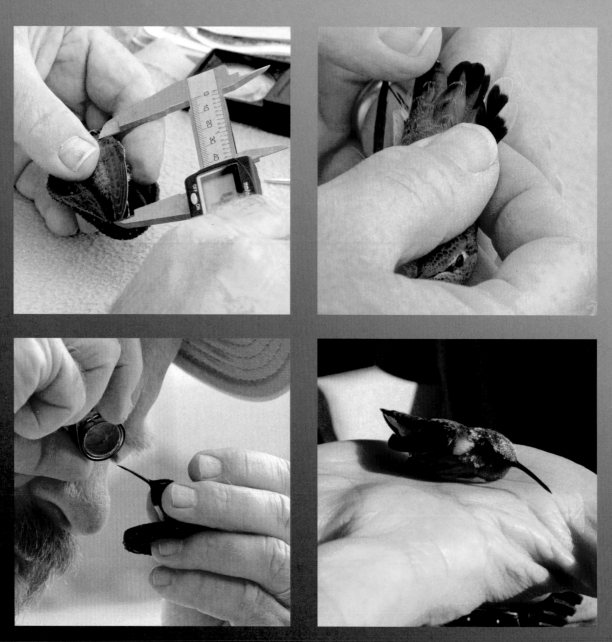

An ***ornithologist*** is a scientist who studies birds. An ***ornithologist*** studying hummingbirds will learn all they can about their behavior, habitat and physical characteristics. The government allows ***ornithologists*** to capture hummingbirds and attach a tiny numbered band to their leg. They will note the birds' size, age, sex and condition as well as where it was caught. When recaptured ***ornithologists*** can learn how far the hummingbird has traveled and how old it is.

Pollen

Pollen is part of a flower.
It helps new flowers grow.
Hummingbirds are quite useful
spreading pollen as they go.

P p

Hummingbirds play an important part in the pollination process. **Pollen** is the material needed for plants to form seeds to grow another plant. Small grains of **pollen** must be transferred from one flower to another for this to happen. When a hummingbird dips its bill inside a flower to sip the nectar, it will often pick up **pollen** on its bill or head. Those small grains of **pollen** will fall off inside the next flower they go to helping new seeds to grow.

Q q

Quiet

Have you heard loud crows or magpies
holler, screech and squawk?
Sweet hummingbirds are quiet,
softly chirping when they talk.

Hummingbirds compared with other wild birds are **quiet.** They do not have a well-known bird song like other birds. In flight, you can hear the hum of their wings moving up to 80 beats per second. Sometimes you can hear a chirp or two as a hummingbird nears a feeder or flower. If two hummingbirds are fighting over a food source, they make a series of rapid chirps to send the other bird away.

R r

Regurgitate

When baby hummingbirds get hungry,
their mothers will find them food.
Then they will digest it
and regurgitate it – eww!

Baby hummingbirds cannot feed themselves. They depend on their mothers to digest nectar and bugs for them. Then the mother **regurgitates** (spits up) the mixture into the babies throats with her long bill. A mother hummingbird will feed her babies about every 20 minutes. It takes a lot of energy for a mother hummingbird to find enough food for her babies and feed them so often.

S s

Symmetry

If you look into a mirror
you'll see another you.
Symmetry in nature
matches left and right, it's true!

In nature, a pattern of equal parts that are a mirror image is called **symmetry**. This **symmetry** can be seen in pinecones, snowflakes, butterfly wings or in a maple leaf. In hummingbirds, their wing and tail feathers often show us the beauty of **symmetry** with each side looking identical to the other. Can you fynd three other things in nature that have **symmetry**?

Torpor

Have you seen hummingbirds in torpor?
They seem to hibernate.
Resting to save their energy,
they sleep in this peaceful state.

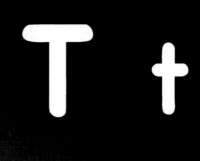

When hummingbirds need to rest, they go into a sleep-like hibernation called *torpor*. They conserve energy during *torpor* as their body temperature and heart rate drops very low. They will puff out their feathers, perch on a hidden branch or even hang upside down. It is hard to find a hummingbird in *torpor*. It takes 20 to 60 minutes for a hummingbird to wake up. Then they are very hungry.

U u

Unafraid

Hummingbirds can be quite feisty.
They are bold and unafraid.
Get too near their flower
an enemy you'll have made.

Hummingbirds are territorial. They believe a nearby feeder or group of flowers is their personal dining area. Quick to fend off invaders, hummingbirds are **unafraid** to aggressively fight for their food source. They will dart and dive close to an uninvited guest, warning them to go away. Sometimes they will challenge another bird with their long, pointy bills using it like a sword.

V v

Vertebrates

Hummingbirds are vertebrates
with a backbone and a brain.
Like dogs, frogs and crocodiles
they're vertebrates just the same.

Hummingbirds belong to a larger group of animals called **vertebrates**, meaning they have a backbone. Additional characteristics of **vertebrates** are they have internal skeletons and nervous systems with a brain and spinal cord. Imagine all that in such a tiny bird. **Vertebrates** include over 65,000 different species of birds, mammals, amphibians and reptiles.

Wings

Most birds flap their **wings** to fly from place to place. Hummer **wings** are different, rotating at a blurring pace.

Hummingbirds move their *wings* in a unique way. Unlike other birds that flap their *wings* up and down, hummingbirds rotate their *wings*. They are able to do this because they have a ball and socket joint in their shoulder. Their *wings* will beat 60 to 80 times per second as they rotate 180 degrees (a half circle). If diving, their *wings* can beat up to 200 times a second. Wow! That's fast!

X Marks the Spot

Hummingbird nests are built in odd places
camouflaged and hard to see.
X-Marks the Spot in these photos.
Are any hidden in a big green tree?

Hummingbirds are masters at camouflaging their nests. They will often select very unusual places to call home. Besides the usual bushes and trees, hummingbirds build nests in wire fences, outdoor lights, patio decorations and in unfriendly, prickly plants. *X-Marks the Spot* where these hummingbirds thought their babies would be safe from

Y y

Yellow Jackets

A hummingbird will get quite angry
fighting **yellow-jackets** or bees.
Chasing them from their food saying,
"Go away, leave it alone won't you please?"

Hummingbirds often deal with uninvited guests at their feeders. Bees, wasps, hornets and *yellow-jackets* will put up a fearless fight to maintain ownership of a feeder. Hummingbirds equally aggressive and unwilling to share take on these intruders. Eventually the hummingbird flies off to another flower and may return later hoping the annoying insect is gone.

Zigzag

Swooping up, down, all around,
a dance male hummingbirds do.
Zigzag patterns left then right
for a female they hope to woo.

Z z

At certain times of the year, especially during mating season, male hummingbirds try to impress a female with their acrobatic flying. Zooming high into the air in a *zigzag* pattern, then diving straight down, a male hummingbird is hopeful his flying skills will catch the eye of the nearby female. Have you ever seen a hummingbird, *zigzag* around, swooping up, diving down? They certainly get your attention.

HUMMINGBIRD FUN FACTS

- There are more than 340 hummingbird species in the world.

- Hummingbirds were named for the humming noise their wings make when they fly.

- Hummingbirds cannot smell but have great eyesight. They like red flowers because they are easy to see.

- Hummingbirds can hear better than humans.

- Hummingbird feet are very small and rarely used to walk. They are good for perching on limbs or scratching.

- Hummingbirds on average have 940 feathers.

- The Bee hummingbird found in Cuba is the smallest of the species measuring only 2.25 inches long.

- Hummingbirds lay the smallest eggs of any birds. They measure less than ½ inch long.

- An average hummingbird's heart beats 1,200 beats per minute while an average person's heart beats 75 beats per minute.

- Normal body temperature for a hummingbird is 107 degrees while normal for humans is 98.6.

- The average lifespan of a hummingbird is 3 to 4 years. Some have lived up to 12 years.

- Hummingbirds are super smart and can remember all the flowers they have been to and how much time they need to refill with nectar.

- Hummingbirds are found only in the Western Hemisphere.

- Ecuador has the largest number of different hummingbird species.

- Some hummingbirds migrate about 500 miles from their summer to winter homes and back.

- The Rufous hummingbird flies about 3,000 miles twice a year between Alaska and Mexico.

RESOURCES

Websites

http://www.sandiegozoo.org/animalbytes/t-hummingbird.html

http://www.birdwatching-bliss.com/hummingbirds.html

http://www.audubon.org/educate/kids

http://www.hummingbirdsociety.org

http://www.hummingbirds.net

http://www.sabo.org

http://www.biglearning.com/treasurebirds.htm

http://www.enchantedlearning.com/subjects/birds/printouts/Hummerprintout.shtml

Books

Aziz, Laurel. *Hummingbirds: A Beginner's Guide*. Firefly Books, 2002.

Biel, Timothy. *Zoobooks: Hummingbirds*. Wildlife Education, 1996.

Kelly, Irene. *It's a Hummingbird's Life*. Holiday House, 2003.

Rauzon, Mark J. *Hummingbirds*. Franklin Watts, 1997.

Sill, Cathryn. *About Hummingbirds: A Guide for Children*. Peachtree, 2013.

Wynne, Patricia J. *Birds: Nature's Magnificent Flying Machines*. Charlesbridge, 2003.

Other

Arizona-Sonora Desert Museum, Tucson, AZ

http://www.desertmuseum.org

Merry Bradshaw is a former educator, now free-lance writer. She wrote educational material for *National Geographic's Explorer Magazines*. Her poetry is part of *Poetry Friday's* anthology, *Celebrations*. She was a winner in the National Federation of Press Women's Communications Contest for *Writing for the Web*. Her writing has been featured in Harvard's Graduate School of Education Newsletter. The west is her home, always enjoying the outdoors and whatever nature presents. Merry Bradshaw is married and lives in southern Nevada.

David Boyarski is a self-taught nature photographer who only got serious about photography when he retired in 2011. His favorite subjects are hummingbirds and humpback whales, two subjects he is not likely to photograph together. The images of hummingbirds used in this book were captured on the eastern slopes of Colorado, in southern Nevada and near Nanegalito, Ecuador. David and his wife live in southern Nevada and enjoy traveling to locations abundant with wildlife.

27745486R10022

Made in the USA
Columbia, SC
14 October 2018